THE STRENGHT OF PUSSY-WAYS TO GET YOUR MAN SUBMIT TO YOUR EVERY REQUEST

TABLE OF CONTENTS

Introduction:

Ambiguous dating and affair recommendation book, "The Force of the Pussy", shares 4 powerful insider facts that will remake any lady into the sort major areas of strength, the lady that can easily get what she needs from men; including the

adoration, regard, and relationship she wants. In this book, you'll learn important examples that will show you how to...

♥ Flip the switch in your female cerebrum, so you can beat men unexpectedly...

♥ Have men arranging to date you and frantic for your consideration...

♥ Figure out how to move past a separation, mend from a messed up heart, and at no point ever be miserable over a man in the future!

♥ Turn into the sort of lady that deserves admiration from men

Get what you need from men and have a great time while making it happen! This book has

enabled ladies and decisively completely changed them and connections by significantly impacting how they contemplate men and dating... and it can change your life as well!

Chapter 1: Beating a man at his game

We know how he works; in some cases, we're mindful that he's a player, yet we turn out to be played.

His game areas of strength are'; so enchanting and attractive, and he generally knows the perfect comment.

He prevails with regards to causing you to accept his every word and causing you to feel unique. **Before long, you wind up in a maze of falsehoods, not realizing the exit plan or what the genuine truth is.**

What's more, when he shows you his real essence, you at last understand that he defeated you.

Not this time. Assume command and make him fixated on you with Captivation Contents.

Now there are five steps to achieve our goal

Step 1: Ignore him

Players are accustomed to drawing consideration the second they enter a club. To play him, first, you need to definitely stand out, and trust me, overlooking him is the ideal method for getting it done. Yet, be cautious you would rather not appear to be discourteous. What you want to do is to amiably overlook him. causing him to feel as though you're not keen on squandering your energy on him and that he

needs to put in more effort if he has any desire to dazzle you let him in on that you're not a simple catch.

Try not to be on backup and continually drop intends to meet with him show him that you're in charge and that you esteem your time beyond what his until he can substantiate himself the hour of day. He needs to work and invest the energy for you if he doesn't make it happen. Saves everybody a boatload of time to have stayed free.

There might be one time when you'll have to act keen on him, just to draw him in, however after that assuming he expresses hey to you scarcely answer. Act occupied, look uninterested, and decline to show that you see or hear anything from him.

Step 2: Flirt with other guys.

Ok indeed, old fashioned round of desire. you showed no interest in investing energy with him no premium in hearing his commendations and jokes and you are right there, having a ton of fun with different folks, snickering at their jokes and becoming flushed at their remarks. I believe there's compelling reason need to depict how completely hopeless he will feel when you do this.

Be that as it may, don't wrongly make it clear you need his consideration or probably it won't work.

Try not to take a gander at him while you're playing with different folks show him that he's good and gone.

So cause him to feel terrible or desirous, spending time with different folks mimmight be your pass to do so nobody is safe to their sesentiments so making him to see that you couldn't care less about him ought to assist

with placing him in line.

Go out, have a great time, eat, drink, and dance, have some good times, and don't restrict yourself as a result of him, however, make source he sees every last bit of it.

Yet again be mindful so as not to appear too coy, barely enough to light the flash of desire in him, he will get the opposition he wants and will get the opportunity to demonstrate the amount of an astonishing person he is (not).

Step 3: Stay immune to his charm.

He's accustomed to having the consideration of the multitude of ladies around him, however show him that you are not succumbing to that call him Romeo or call the ladies around him his sweethearts.

This person lives on his appeal; it's one of the

main characteristics he has that works. So he will do his best to engage as he would prefer into your jeans.

All things being equal, show him that you do not succumb into to his appeal. It's an old demonstration. He should concoct an at the ornate system if he has any desire to make you succumb to him once he becomes fixated, the next move is up to you and you've beaten the person at playing his own game.

Step 4: Criticize him in front of others.

This could be interesting, so you should be key And subtel about it. While you're conversing with companions or family, delicately poke a fun at how he has a blemish you realize he's uncertain about it ensure it's something you to have seen about him Or things he haphazardly told you, be that as it may, it ought not to be a secret he imparted to you. do whatever it takes not to sound annoying or designing also.

Step 5: **Maintain the mystery**

Try not to give out a lot of data about yourself. Give him barely enough to respond to the inquiry, however insufficient that he would have the total story. No referencing of exes, of your fantasies, expectations, and fears.

The main thing to do is to stay secretive and by doing all of this, you will prevail in it. Continuously remember that players are accustomed to getting all that they need, and when they see that this time they can't have it, they will go off the deep end.

In this way, in the event that he gets some information about your day, give him something endless and get some information about his day.

Try not to be very easy to read, ensure he needs to remain around you so he can get to know a greater amount of you. It's adequately not to simply be subtle. Be secretive too. Beside the looks and the grins, don't chip in much data about yourself.

On the off chance that buts some information about your day, shrug and grin cautiously and get some information about his day. Never discuss your ex, your expectations, and fears, what you like in a person, or how you copied your tongue that morning by slurping your espresso excessively quickly. Make him think about what's truly at the forefront of your

thoughts by talking ambiguously. Make him figure out what your identity and you're about, and he'll try to sort you out like a jigsaw puzzle.

Bonus: Avoid too many emoticons

Stay away from such a large number of emojis

To know how to message a person right, don't overdo it on the grinning and winking emoticon. Loads of individuals, especially men, find an excess of emoticons somewhat unpleasant. It likewise can exhibit an absence of capacity to express anything for yourself.

It's OK to message him and use emoticons however downplay them. *more words, less emojis*

Chapter 2: understanding yourself.

Having a profound comprehension of ourselves it's fundamental for all that we do. He is indispensable for our prosperity it's crucial seeing close, true connections, and it's essential for making significant satisfying fulfilling life.

how well do you column yourself a few times the you could end up doing things despite the fact that you are not exactly certain why your psyche controls an immense measure of your way of behaving and in this manner the thinking behind a significant number of our choice in life can be covered in secret. In any case, in the event that you know how to look you can

acquire a more noteworthy comprehension of yourself. for what reason did you conclude that you do, what fulfills you on how you could change for better?

As you stay aware of everything happening in your life the obligations, the commitments, and, surprisingly, the interruptions, there will be times when you thoroughly search in the mirror and battle to perceive yourself. Where did I go? How might I comprehend myself better? You ask meandering how you have wound up where you are. How did my arrangements for the future wind up so... messed up?

At the point when you don't carve out opportunity to comprehend yourself and who you are a feeling of independence debilitates. you become effortlessly impacted and driven into a way of life that doesn't address what your identity is.

At the point when you assume you have a very

decent handle on what really matters to you, you find yourself accomplishing something shockingly bizarre.

or then again is it? perhaps you don't know yourself as well as you suspected. perhaps the more odd piece of you is as yet a secret to the piece of it that manages everything.

anyway, your inward creep continue to appear.

I don't know whether to wipe the slate clean with it or exercise authority over it.

Many individuals miss the mark on mindfulness to respond to the accompanying inquiries who are you when no other person is near? where do you feel generally great and what circumstance causes your hair to stand on end? do you have any idea why this is the situation? Do you comprehend yourself and why you are how you are?

Presently I'll show you five different ways each

of the five significant ways of understanding yourselves better.

Steps 1 Take a personality test.

Step 2 evaluate your strength and weakness.

Step 3 examine your priorities.

Step 4. Be honest with yourself.

Step 5 develop your self-awareness.

STEP 1: TAKE A PERSONALITY TEST

the main thing you can do to acquire a more noteworthy comprehension of yourself is to get a few objective evaluations. You can ask individuals you know, But their Experience of you could lead them to the very predisposition that you have hearing some goal point of view will give you a more precise picture and lead you to consider a few things you probably won't actually have considered. There are various laid out tests that you can take to find out about the various parts of yourself me.

- Myers-briggs Personality type hypothesis says that all individuals have one of 16 distinct essential character can't foresee how you can collaborate with individuals, the sort of relational issue and strength that you have, on what sort of climate you live and work in best.
- In the event that you are attempting to comprehend what makes you blissful and how you ought to manage your life, consider taking a lifelong test. These sort of tests can assist you with concluding what you could find the most fulfilling, generally founded on your character

and how you help fun.

Assuming you have never taken the Myers Briggs type marker (MBTI)

Check it out.

It doesn't take long, and it can uncover things about you that could have notice however haven't exactly pondered.

Perhaps you need a few pieces of information about what kind of work would cause you to feel generally invigorated and for the most part feeling yourself.

those hints are only one of the advantages of getting to know your character attributes. You don't need to concur with each detail in your sort portrayal.

Step 2 Evaluates Your Strengths And Weaknesses

You can come to a superior comprehension of what your identity and is generally critical to you by thinking about your assets and shortcomings recognized by your companions, family, and colleagues. The things that they see that you don't can perceive you a ton about yourself and how you see yourself.

• Instances of qualities incorporate assurance,, definitiveness commitment, self-restraint, care, tolerance, Diplomacy, relational abilities, and creative mind or imagination.

• Illustration of shortcoming incorporate close mindedness, egotistical Ness, trouble seeing reality, judgment of others and issues with control.

Step 3: Examine Your Priorities.

What do you believe is most significant

throughout everyday life and in your everyday

communication can educate you a ton regarding yourself.

Contemplate your needs, contrast them with the needs of others you regard, say regarding you obviously you should be available to the possibility that you probably won't have your needs in the best request (Many individuals don't), Which can likewise show you a ton yourself.

• Assuming your home were burning to the ground, how might you respond? What might You save? It's astounding the way that fire uncovered our needs.

Regardless of whether you would save something pragmatic, similar to your duty record, that actually expresses something about you (Most likely that you like to be ready and not meets opposition throughout everyday life)

• One more method for determining what your needs are is to envision that somebody you love was transparently reprimanded for something that you don't uphold (Suppose, they are lesbians yet you disagree with the way of life).

do you uphold them? Safeguard them? How? What might you say? Our activities notwithstanding peer analysis And conceivable excluding can uncover our needs.

• some adequate needs that individuals frequently need to incorporate cash, family, sex, regard, security, solidness, material belongings, and solaces.

Step 4: Being Honest With Yourself

Where you receive a message from somebody you are intentionally unwinding from, your heart no longer leaps for happiness, rather there's little foreboding shadow or a transitory feeling

of distress. Pay attention to your divine beings. In the event that you fell "meh" About a person or thing, don't enjoy it.

on the off chance that you feel a feeling of fear about showing up at a party, don't go assuming that you burn through a portion of your effort on individuals and things who don't give pleasure, you will be depleted and thusly become unscrupulous.

Yet, legitimate do you try and like who you are the point at which you are with individuals or in circumstances that chokes out you? Pay attention to your divine beings. It will assist with guiding you to more profound comprehension of yourself.

We like to ourselves much more than we might want to contemplate something. We'll grab imagine that we pursued a few sketchy decisions for respectable or sensible reasons,

in any event, when we were simply being

malicious or lethargic. Both stowing away from the genuine explanation for our intentions doesn't help us change and form into better individuals recollect.

There's no reason for line to yourself regardless of whether you find insights about yourself. that you truly could do without this main offers you the chance to take those issues head on rather than simply imagining.

Step 5: Develop Your Self-awareness

We have inward outer mindfulness and interior mindfulness incorporates information on our ethics and upsides of specified previously.

Our magnificent mindfulness is the way we remember we are seen by others.

Do you have any idea how you run over others? You might think you are fun and happy, though your most treasured may think that you are grating and discourteous.

how truly do individuals answer you? How viable is your correspondence?

Have some genuine discussion with loved ones, do you depict your genuine self to the outside.

CHAPTER 3: Controlling Your Emotions

Feeling are strong your state of mind decide how you communicate with individuals, how you manage difficulties, and how you spend your times.

Gaming command over your feelings will assist you with turning out to be intellectually more

grounded. Luckily, anybody can turn out to be

better at directing their feelings. Very much like

some other abilities dealing with your feelings requires practice and devotion figure out how to acknowledge and handle your feelings in a none critical manner.

Keep even headed and pay attention to your accomplices particularly during warmed contention at last, attempt to foster a more uplifting perspective so you feel more sure about yourself and your relationship.

Feelings it's undeniably true's that quite possibly of

the most introductory variable drive us. The most effective method to get a grip on your feelings in a relationship can either make your or break things for yourself as well as your accomplice.

Feelings in relationship different with regards to power. They permit you to feel and investigate

the broadest scope of feeling you haven't felt previously.

From falling head over heels to your most memorable significant battles, it with a people accomplice that you will encounter a hurricane of feelings.

You'll encounter bliss, love, dread, outrage, irritation, uneasiness, frailty, hopelessness, disdain, thus substantially more.

So I would be giving you one strategy for how to put your feelings on check.

Processing your emotions:

Now when it comes to processing emotion there are 3steps to do that.

STEP 1: IDENTIFY YOUR EMOTIONS CAREFULLY AND SPECIFICALLY

Before you can manage gloomy feelings, you want to recognize them, envision you're composing a report on your feelings and you

should be pretty much as itemized as conceivable you shouldn't just ponder sort of feeling, however the force of that feelings, as well.

• "Upset" is a dubious method for depicting your close to home state, dig further to track down a

more unambiguous identifier, as "profoundly frustrated".

• Instead of saying you feel " great", you could portray yourself as feeling "delighted" or "loose".

• Recall that your are not your feelings as feelings is impermanent circumstances, similar as a climate framework going through. Rather than saying "I'm furious", say " I feel furious at this moment".

STEP 2: FIGURE OUT WHY YOU'RE FEELING THIS WAY.

Whenever you've recognized and noticed your feelings, it's the ideal opportunity for a little investigator work. Take care not to project sentiments emerging from your issues on top of your accomplice.

Pose yourself a couple of inquiries to figure out

where the sentiments are coming from. For instance, what precisely set off your response? Could it be said that you are frantic on the

grounds that you feel slighted by your part or companion or does your outrage have more to do with a harsh day at work?

This can assist you with sorting out your inclination like your sentiments is shared or something more serious. It will likewise assist you with talking yourself through your sentiments when you feel them. Is this

fascination? Desire when you feel a warm blush begins to spread across your face or a comparative inclination, recognize the feelings, and emphatically talk yourself through it.

• assuming you're feeling desirous, inquire as to whether your envy is the consequence of past damages. Contemplate your relationship, with family, companions, and exes do any injuries from these connections make sense of your ongoing sensations of desire?

• "I'm simply anxious in light of the fact that I believe he's charming, I've been around other adorable young men and it's no biggie. I will be alright".

• " I realize that I now and again get restless around him. Yet, that is okay, individuals at times get restless around pounds. I will do my best far.

STEPS 3: BREATH IN DEEPLY TO CALM YOURSELF

At the point when your feelings move away from your breathing will frequently gain out of influence a swell, intensifying your sensations of stress and nervousness. Remove this winding when your vibe it occurring by taking a few body. On the off chance that you would be able, attempt an intentional profound breathing strategy for the best arrangement.

At the point when unmistakable inclinations take steps to overpower you, it is normal to answer unwittingly by taking shallow relaxes. To work on your breathing, for a couple inhales attempt to focus just to your breathe in and breathe out this will reestablish hour cognizant regard for your body and it's requirement for full, realxed during a strained contention.

• to attempt this procedure in front of the pack one hand on your chest and the other beneath your rib confine. Breathe in leisurely and profoundly feel your lungs and midsection grow as you fill them with air.

• hold the relax for 1 or 2 seconds then leisurely delivery the breath through your mouth go for the gold full breath.

CHAPTER 4: UNDERSTANDING MEN

Heard the platitude "Men are from Mars and ladies are from Venus?" Even on the off chance that you haven't, you may be feeling like you and the folks you know are on totally various planets. Not figuring out your accomplice, specifically, can be debilitating, and it can prompt a ton of personal unrest, as well. While each man is unique, there are a couple of things you can remember as you endeavor to figure out the men in your day to day existence and reinforce your connections.

Now I would explain how men act and react to certain situation and usual habits.

Men Covers True Feelings With Anger

Men will now and again change over more "female" feelings into outrage or fury. As a general rule, he might be feeling miserable, powerless, or even humiliated, yet he doesn't have the foggiest idea how to say it. Assuming you notice that he's consistently furious, have a go at getting some information about his feelings of anxiety or how he's inclination.

Outrage is the one feeling that is socially "satisfactory" for men to feel.

Men frequently feel like in the event that they express anything more, they'll be viewed as "silly" or "not masculine enough."

Most men don't veil their feelings deliberately; rather, they've figured out how to do it through cultural tensions and assumptions.

This can prompt disappointing discussions. Nonetheless, men are generally instructed not to discuss their feelings, so holding through words can be intense for them. All things considered, they could get a kick out of the chance to have

discussions with an obvious reason or issue to solve.

For instance, on the off chance that you're having a discussion about your relationship, your accomplice could experience difficulty communicating what you mean to him. This can be difficult to hear, however it's most likely in light of the fact that he's not used to discussing his sentiments.

However, your accomplice might communicate his sentiments in alternate ways. In the event that he brings you blossoms or prepares you your #1 supper, he may be attempting to communicate his adoration for you without saying it straightforwardly.

Most men haven't gotten the opportunity to deal with their sentiments. He might find it more straightforward to record his contemplations and sentiments and show them to you or send them in a message. On the off chance that he has a very difficult stretch distinguishing his feelings, a psychological well-being proficient can be helpful.

Care rehearses, similar to reflection

and yoga, can assist him with managing his feelings in a solid manner. You could take a stab at doing these exercises together so he doesn't feel alone.

In the event that both of you are attempting to impart about your feelings, have a go at holding a week after week registration where you discuss any issues in the relationship.

This additionally implies that he could require additional opportunity to handle his feelings. Assuming he says he really wants space or to give him time, you ought to regard his

desires.

Pessimistic feelings, similar to trouble, outrage, and agony, can be difficult to process. A few men will pull out from their loved ones as opposed to discussing what they're feeling. Assuming you notice this, you can attempt to consult with him about what's happening, yet he might require a chance to manage everything on his own.

This could appear as though him requiring longer hours at work, drinking more liquor, investing more energy away from home, or acting

wildly.

The best thing to do is to tell him that you're here to talk at whatever point he's prepared. Assuming you attempt to drive him to open dependent upon you, he could pull out significantly further. This is particularly normal after a profound trial, similar to the departure of a friend or family member.

Men Find It Hard Asking For Help

You might bring to the table to help

before they inquire. This incorporates tackling errands, searching for lost things, or in any event, planning physical checkups. Assuming you notice that he's battling, have a go at offering help if possible.

Take a stab at expressing something like, "Hello, do you want assistance searching for your keys? I assume I saw them on the table yesterday." Or, "Did you be able to call your primary care physician? I can find the telephone number for you assuming that you want it."

Men may likewise find it hard to

acknowledge your assistance, regardless of whether they truly need it. You can keep on offering your help tenderly however immovably so they know that you're here assuming you want them.

He Might Try To Solve All Your Problems

Since this is normal from a ton of men, he could think you anticipate it, as well. This

can be disappointing when you're simply attempting to vent about a terrible day or an irritating colleague, so you ought to be clear and tell him precisely what you need before you start talking.

For instance, you could say, "I will recount to you a story now, yet I don't require guidance. I simply have to talk it through with

somebody."

Attempting to take care of everybody's concerns can be

debilitating, so it's not great for him, all things considered!

BONUS CHAPTER: PLAYING MIND GAMES WITH A MAN

Men playing mind games in a relationship can baffle. Additionally, men can adore and prize you at one

second and act totally uninterested the following second, which could considerably more irritate.

A few examples of psyche games that men play are:

1.A person might be keen on you and continually texts you. Notwithstanding, they may abruptly go off the radar when you respond to them.

2.You are with your man in a gathering, and he begins playing with different ladies to cause you to feel desirous.

3.Your person may frequently condemn your dressing style, while others acclaim you for the equivalent.

Men are typically extremely clear about their affections for somebody. Yet, assuming your man likes to keep you hanging without giving any obvious sign of how he feels about you, then, at that point, here are a few signs that he is playing mind games.

1.Hot and cold way of behaving:

You used to continually message

each other for quite a long time before he unexpectedly cut contact with practically no advance notice or reason. You stress and can't help thinking about what has been going on with him. In any case, a couple of days or weeks after the fact, he returns with an explanation that sounds crazy to you. This is known as the 'hot and cold' conduct. You realize he has been on the web, just he hasn't informed you. In the event that he does this frequently, realize without a doubt that he is essentially playing with you.

2.Not great as his words:

You go out on the town with this person, and you both appear to live it up together. Not long after the date, he texts you, requesting to meet him soon. You consent to it and afterward hang tight for him to ask you out, however his message won't ever come. Fed up with pausing, you text him getting some information about the date. He presently boasts over the way that you were sitting tight for him, and are keen on him. He fundamentally showed interest and

kept you hanging just so you could pursue him.

3.Comments on your looks:

A couple of gatherings with this person, and you will hear him express something like, 'You ought to sort out more frequently to look more alluring' or 'You ought to attempt a hair styling that will make your face look slimmer.' When a man feels you are excessively great for him, he will initially attempt to kill your

confidence by

acting not interested in your engaging quality. With such remarks, he believes that you should accept that you are not so alluring as you naturally suspect and that he is the one agreeing to a split the difference in this relationship. This is a shrewd stunt that demonstrates he expects to play mind games.

4.Ghosts you a few times:

This person calls you, makes elaborate arrangements for the afternoon, and lets you know he will be there, yet never turns up. You attempt to contact him, however he is inaccessible. A couple of days after the fact, he will show up saying 'sorry' and promising to make up. He could conceivably make up with you however will doubtlessly leave you in a reel in the future. You feel he is hanging a carrot just to have you pursued him.

5.Toys with your feelings:

When together, he could frequently get some

information about him. You hold nothing back from him, sharing your adoration and friendship for him. You could anticipate that he should talk about his thoughts for you, however all things considered, he will change the point. Assuming that he is somebody excessively brimming with himself, he could try and prod you by expressing his dream of dating one more young lady notwithstanding knowing how you feel for him. Such

men appreciate prodding ladies and shaking their feelings, and frequently do as such with practically no culpability.

6.Keeps contact just for sex:

You notice that this person you are dating is AWOL the vast majority of the days however abruptly gives you consideration when he really

wants sex. He won't try to answer to your directive for quite a long time however will unexpectedly appear to be dynamic and inspired by you. He could try and dishonestly guarantee you of his affections for you, however his activities never back up his words. If so with you, then he is utilizing you. Take off from him beyond

what many would consider possible.

7.Does not acquaint you with his loved ones:

If a person acquaints you with his family, it implies he could be not kidding about you. On the off chance that he doesn't, then, at that point,

he is most likely not. He might welcome you to spend time with his person pack yet won't ever take you to meet his folks or kin or anybody essential to him. He could be doing so on the grounds that he isn't completely certain of his affections for you.

He gives you looks into his life just to keep you snared

until he finds somebody better.

8.Makes you keep absurd guidelines:

He makes rules for the both of you that could cause you to feel like you are his filthy mystery. For example, both of you can't clasp hands in

broad daylight, or you can't distribute pictures of both of you together via virtual entertainment. He might do this since he could be dating different ladies at the same time and doesn't have any desire to cause problems.

9.Treats you terrible before others:

Your person unexpectedly changes into a disparaging beast who passes scornful comments about you. Folks frequently prefer to show mastery in a relationship however putting their accomplice down is the most horrendously terrible thing to do. They might try and claim to order you to intrigue others. On the off

chance that your person does this, you better talk with him about it before it goes crazy.

10.Never texts you first:

No matter how well both of you hit it off face to face, this person never texts you first. When together, he gives you

the feeling that he loves you and appreciates your conversation, yet he never steps up to the plate and text or makes arrangements. In the event that a kid is doing this to you, fail to remember him and continue on since he is undoubtedly being pleasant to you and truly has no heartfelt interests.

www.ingramcontent.com/pod-product-compliance
Lightning Source LLC
LaVergne TN
LVHW080558160826
845677LV00010B/1891

9798849890821